James Freeman Clarke

The fourth Gospel

The question of its origin stated and discussed

James Freeman Clarke

The fourth Gospel
The question of its origin stated and discussed

ISBN/EAN: 9783337281366

Printed in Europe, USA, Canada, Australia, Japan

Cover: Foto ©Thomas Meinert / pixelio.de

More available books at **www.hansebooks.com**

THE FOURTH GOSPEL

THE QUESTION OF ITS ORIGIN STATED
AND DISCUSSED

BY

JAMES FREEMAN CLARKE

BOSTON
GEO. H. ELLIS, 141 FRANKLIN STREET
1886

THE PROBLEM OF THE FOURTH GOSPEL.

THE problem of the Fourth Gospel is this; how could a Gospel proceeding from John, one of the companions and apostles of Jesus, give a view of his character and life differing in many ways from that of the other three evangelists? On the other hand, if it was *not* written by John, but by some later author, how could it have been universally received in the early Church as genuine and authentic, and no trace of opposition to it be found in all Christendom, from Egypt to Gaul? If it gives us a Gnostic Jesus or an Alexandrian Jesus, and not the Jesus of Palestine, its universal reception is all the more unaccountable.

This is the problem which has been discussed in Germany and elsewhere since the time of Ferdinand Christian Baur, and is yet an unsettled question. I shall give the arguments on both sides, especially those which proceed from such opponents of the Johannine origin of the Gospel as Baur himself, John James Tayler and Albert Réville; and, more recently, as they are summed up by Holtzmann in his *Historical and Critical Introduction to the New Testament* (Freiburg, 1885), and by Dr. Abbott in the Encyclopædia Britannica.

We will first consider the objections to the authorship of John, as given some years since in the very able work of Mr. Tayler, formerly principal of Manchester New College, London. This book is called *An Attempt to ascertain the Character of the Fourth Gospel*. But it is not so much an examination as an argument. It is a fair and honest attempt to disprove the apostolic anthorship of the Gospel; and it sums up the reasons for rejecting it, as given by Baur and others down to 1867. In considering Mr. Tayler's arguments, we shall know the strongest points that could be made against the received opinion at the time when Mr. Tayler wrote; and perhaps, even now, there is no one book which states and summarizes them so well.

I.

Mr. Tayler first describes the evident difference between the three Synoptic Gospels and the Fourth, as regards the scene of Christ's labors, the form of his teachings, the events mentioned, and the resulting view of the character of Christ himself. He thinks that John's Gospel is not so much another as a different Gospel from those of the Synoptics. Considering it impossible that the Fourth Gospel and the Apocalypse should have been written by the same author, he decides in favor of the authenticity of the latter. The references to the Apostle John in Scripture and ecclesiastical tradition show, in his opinion, that John belonged to the Jewish section of the Christian Church, to which, plainly, the author of the Fourth Gospel does not belong. The external testimonies to the apostolic authorship of the Gospel do not begin to be satisfactory till toward the end of the second century. The doctrine of the Logos, he thinks, could not have been blended so intimately with Christianity at an early period as it appears in this book. In the apologists of the second century, indeed, he finds this Logos doctrine fully accepted; but, in the writings of Paul, instead of the "Logos" we have the "Spirit." But his chief reason for rejecting the Gospel as apostolic is from its position in regard to the time of the Last Supper. The three Synoptics place it on the fourteenth of Nisan, on the day of the Passover; but John puts it on the day before, and fixes the crucifixion on the Passover. That the Fourth Gospel is wrong here, Mr. Tayler thinks evident; and that, therefore, it could not be written by John, who was incapable of such a mistake, and whose authority was appealed to in Ephesus in favor of the other date. For such reasons as these, he considers himself compelled to deny the apostolic authorship of the Fourth Gospel. Who was really the writer he is unable to say; but he is convinced that it was some one who was living and writing before the middle of the second century,— certainly before the death of Papias in A.D. 163, and probably after A.D. 135. He differs from Dr. Baur, who considers it of Alexandrine origin, since he regards the uniform tradition of the Church in favor of Ephesus conclusive as to the place of its composition.

The Fourth Gospel, therefore, according to

Mr. Tayler, "belongs to the primitive age of Christianity, and cannot be brought lower than the first half of the second century." Nevertheless, he does not consider it as the work of imposture: partly because it does not speak of John as its author till the last chapter, which he holds to be a later addition; and, also, because the book is really filled with the current of spiritual life which came from Jesus. His work ends with an attempt to show that Baron Bunsen was wrong in saying that, if John's Gospel is not authentic, there can be no historical Christ and no Christian ·Church. On the other hand, Mr. Tayler asserts that Christianity is not damaged by the results of this criticism, and that we lose nothing in discovering that the Fourth Gospel was not the work of an apostle, but of an unknown writer at Ephesus, in the second century.

Let us next consider the subsequent history of this question, and the present state of opinion among the critics of Germany, as given in Holtzmann's recent book (1885). Holtzmann is one of the leading theologians of the school of Baur; and, like Mr. Tayler and Réville, he rejects the Johannine authorship. We may thus depend on his giving full weight to the objections to the received opinion.

Holtzmann, though admitting that the Fourth Gospel has a right to be accepted as a Gospel, gives the following reasons for his own view.

The prologue to John contains the only passage in the Gospel which treats of the pre-existence and eternal being of Jesus, and differs wholly in its tone from the Synoptic Gospels (Matthew, Mark, and Luke,— called *Synoptic* because all taking the same view of the course of events in the life of Jesus). In John, the historic element yields to the philosophic and supernatural one. New historic facts are introduced, such as the words of the Baptist, the conversations of Jesus with the Jews and his disciples, — characters, places, situations, not in the first three Gospels. In these, the scene of Christ's work is chiefly in Galilee; in John, it is laid at Jerusalem. Various events recorded by the Synoptics are omitted in John, such as the Temptation, the Sermon on the Mount, the Transfiguration, and many of the Synoptic miracles, especially those relating to demoniacal possession. The Synoptics give only one year for the public life of Jesus, but John requires more. Moreover, the events in the Fourth Gospel are for the sake of introducing the conversations, not for their own sake, as in the first three Gospels. Instead of popular parables, John's Christ teaches in allegories. The teaching of Jesus in the Synoptics bears immediately on earthly life and human conduct, that in John on more ideal themes. Jesus, in the Synoptics, teaches moral truth; in John, he inculcates faith in himself. In John, all is in broad contrast of light and shadow, of good and evil, lacking the variety of earthly color which is found in the other narratives. Nor in John do we find any development in the ideas of Jesus, or any trace of growth or of struggle. He is perfect from the first. While the Synoptic Gospels are a collection of single, scarcely connected facts, John's is a rounded whole. It is filled with an element of spiritual life, scarcely to be found in the others. These contrasts are so difficult to explain that Holtzmann thinks the easiest outlet is to suppose the Fourth Gospel not the work of an original apostle, but the fruit of a long development of Grecian thought. But such is the variety of views still existing among the most able critics, that Holtzmann ends by declaring the problem of the Fourth Gospel to be more and more an open question.

If those who attack the authenticity of the

Gospel admit this, its defenders must make a like admission. The time is past when the followers of Baur could declare that the non-apostolic authorship of the Gospel was finally and forever settled, and when the conservatives could pour contempt on every effort to disturb the received tradition. Some *via media* must be found. Those who contend that it is an Alexandrian gnostic Gospel, written in order to change the faith of the Church, are obliged to meet the insuperable difficulty of explaining how such an apocryphal Gospel could be received by the whole Church as authentic, without a ripple of opposition. On the other hand, those who argue that the author was an apostle, who wrote in full harmony with the other evangelists, must find some way to account for the different tone and color of this scripture from the others.

Many of the lesser objections may, no doubt, be easily answered. Supposing it to be dictated by the aged apostle to his inquiring disciples at different times near the close of his life, we can understand why much should be omitted with which they were already familiar, and some things added to supply the deficiencies in existing narratives. These additions would largely consist of the incidents and discussions at Jerusalem, omitted by the Synoptics, who were more interested in events and practical truths than in the profounder topics which would arise in conversation with the rabbis. The remarkable introduction to the Fourth Gospel may indicate that John found around him, in his later days, the germs of the future Gnosticism, and met these tendencies with a larger gnosis. So far from teaching the gnostic doctrine that the "Word," "Life," "Light," etc., were separate æons, emanations from the unknown abyss of being, he asserts that "The Word" was God himself, and not a being derived from him. Consequently (as Ezra Abbot tells us *), "the Christian Fathers, in their contests with the Gnostics, found therein an armory of weapons." Hence, the work could scarcely have emanated from a gnostic writer, as Hilgenfeld and others suppose.

As the main attack came from the school of Baur, so the defence was championed by that of Schleiermacher. Holtzmann says: "The defences of the apostolic origin of the Fourth Gospel rest mostly on the profound work of Lücke (1820-1843) and Bleek (1846). Both were personal friends of Schleiermacher. 'The first waves

* *The Authorship of the Fourth Gospel*, p. 88.

of attack broke against the mighty influence of this theologian.' Against doubts in detail, he maintained the power of the total impression of this Gospel, and declared that Christianity is inexplicable if we rest it solely on the statements of the Synoptics,— an axiom also maintained by Neander, Bunsen, and Ewald."

· Holtzmann describes the present state of opinion as quite unsettled. There are many shades of belief, extending from those who hold fast to the traditional doctrine — as Godet (1876-1877), Keil (1881), Schanz (1885), Westcott (1882), and others — to those who derive the contents of the book from Philo or the Gnostics,— as Wolf, Havet, Réville, and Tayler. Between these extremes are many varieties of critical judgment. Many admit a subjective element by which the thoughts of John are confused in his memory with those of his Master. Some maintain that most of the Gospel is from John, but that some extraneous matter has come in, which may be eliminated by the aid of the Synoptics. Others — especially Beyschlag (1874), A. Ritschl, B. Weiss, and Sanday (1872) — regard the memory of John as furnishing the facts, but as freely treating this material in an historic ideal narrative.

Karl Hase considers the Gospel to have been committed to writing some years after the death of the apostle. Ed. Reuss finds in it a double element, and Schenkel considers the apostle's recollections as furnishing the basis of the work.

In closing his review, Holtzmann admits the extreme difficulty of coming to any perfectly satisfactory opinion. No attempt to reconstruct the Gospel on the principle of a purpose in the writer has succeeded. If Jesus is represented as the divine and supernatural Logos, many traits of human weakness and dependence are also ascribed to him. That he is made a manifestation of the Logos does not necessarily prove his Deity, since Philo (*Vita Mosis*) regards Moses as a manifestation of the Logos. But he inclines to the opinion that the question is best solved by assuming an ideal and real conjunction in the evangel, by which the mystical element may be explained as belonging to the mind of the writer, while the stamp of the Synoptic history may be found in the rest of the story.

The question remains in this condition. As against the authority of the apostle are the differences in the accounts of Jesus as given by the Synoptics, and that in the Fourth Gospel;

but, on the other hand, the moment these are made of importance enough to damage the apostolic authorship, the opposite difficulty of explaining its general reception in the Church is increased. It is incredible that an unknown Gospel, presenting itself in the middle of the second century, claiming the great apostle as its author and giving a new view of Christ, should have been received by the whole Church without the least opposition. The objections rest on internal evidence, for the external evidence is in favor of its authenticity.

One of the most recent, able, and exhaustive examinations of the problem of the Fourth Gospel is to be found in the article by Dr. Edwin A. Abbott, head master of the London schools. This is in the tenth volume of the last edition of the Encyclopædia Britannica, article "Gospels." The author belongs to the freest school of thinkers, and is in evident sympathy with the German and Dutch critics; but he is too thorough a scholar to go all lengths with them in their negations. He sees and admits the marked differences between the Fourth Gospel and the Synoptics, and indicates seventeen points where John thus differs from the Gospels of Matthew, Mark, and Luke. He says it has greater scope than these, is more artistic and complete, is far superior to them in the symmetry of its method, gives more of the purely human traits of the character of Jesus, and often seems to bring him upon the level of pure humanity. It destroys the special privilege of pre-existence by the words, "Did this man sin, that he was born blind?" It is faithful to the spirit rather than the letter of the teaching of Jesus, and cares little for belief founded on wonders. It represents Jesus as always following the intimations of a will higher than his own; makes the signs of his coming not outward, but inward; and, when it does not give the exact words of Jesus, gives us his thoughts. It makes the essence of the resurrection of Jesus spiritual,— a spiritual ascent of the soul in accordance with law, like the sprouting of a seed. Dr. Abbott remarks that the statement of the profound law of the increased influence of the dead on the living can hardly have proceeded from any other than Jesus himself. And, in the last conversations, the spiritual depth of the doctrine goes to show that we have in them much of the Master's own teaching.

As regards the external evidence, Dr. Abbott says that no candid mind can resist the proof that some of the apostolic Fathers (Barnabas, Hermas, Ignatius) used the Fourth Gospel, and that Papias had quoted it before. Hence, he concludes that it was derived from John, and is, as it professes, a "Gospel according to John." But he thinks that it may have been edited by a disciple or a successor, and that John's idiosyncrasy has colored the language attributed to Jesus. But Dr. Abbott gives no support to the view that it was an independent composition, written in the middle of the second century, with the purpose of giving a new view of the character and teaching of Jesus.

II.

We ask next, Which ought to have the most weight in deciding the question of authorship,— the united and unvarying belief of the Church, less than two hundred years after the birth of Christ, or the arguments of criticism, however ingenious, at the present time?

To test this, let us suppose a critic, in the year A.D. 3500, to be examining the question of the authorship of the *Paradise Lost*. He finds,

THE PROBLEM OF THE FOURTH GOSPEL

we will suppose, few references to it before the year 1800; but, at that time, it was universally attributed to John Milton, an eminent English writer of the seventeenth century. Such had continued to be the general belief during all the subsequent centuries. But this critic, on examination, sees much reason for doubting this conclusion. "I find," he says, "other works, in prose, attributed to this same writer,—works of a violent and bitterly controversial character, and wholly different in spirit from the poem. In these, he is a son of Thunder, ready to call down fire from heaven on the heads of his opponents: in this, he is patient under neglect and sorrow. The difference of style also is very great. The prose writings have long, involved, difficult sentences: the verse is luminous, simple, and clear. No person, for example, unbiassed by prejudice, can read the 'Animadversions on the Remonstrant's Defence against Smectymnuus,' and believe the author of this bitter, obscure, and prosaic essay and that of the *Paradise Lost* to be the same person. Take, for example, the following passage, which is a fair specimen of the whole:—

"'The peremptory analysis, that you call it, I believe will be so hardy as once more to unpin your spruce, fastidious oratory, to rumple her laces, her frizzles, and her bobbins, though she wince and fling never so peevishly.

"'*Remonst.*— Those verbal exceptions are but light froth, and will sink alone.

"'*Ans.*— O rare Subtlety, beyond all that Cardan ever dreamed of! when will light froth sink? Here, in your phrase, the same day that heavy plummets will swim alone. Trust this man, readers, if you please, whose divinity would reconcile England with Rome, and his philosophy make friends nature with the chaos, *sine pondere habentia pondus.*

"'*Remonst.*— That scum may be worth taking off, which follows.

"'*Ans.*— Spare your ladle, sir: it will be as the bishop's foot in the broth; the scum will be found upon your own remonstrance.'

"It is evident," our critic might say, "that the man who could write pages of such stuff as this could not be the author of *Paradise Lost*. Which of these, then, was John Milton? Ancient writers declare Milton to have been a Puritan, a friend and secretary of Cromwell, a schoolmaster, the writer of a Latin Dictionary and the History of England. When could he have written the *Paradise Lost?* All tradition agrees that it was not published till 1667. But then he was already fifty-nine years old; and he died seven years after, blind and tormented with the gout. Is it credible that this splendid poem could have been composed at such a time of life and under such circumstances by one who had given all his mature years to politics, sectarian theology, and Latin dictionaries?

"It is true," our thirty-fifth century critic might add, "that the scattering notices of this poem before the nineteenth century do all attribute it to the Puritan John Milton. But it is a suspicious circumstance that one of these writers, named Johnson (who flourished about A.D. 1760), speaks of the 'long obscurity and late reception' of this poem, 'and that it did not break into open view' till the Revolution of 1688. It is also remarkable that the most eminent contemporaries of this writer do not speak of the poem or know of it. Jeremy Taylor, Baxter, Locke, Newton, Leibnitz, all living at the same time, are ignorant of the existence of *Paradise Lost.* If such a great poem had then been published, is it possible that they should not have read it? It is still more singular that the public attention was first called to it forty or fifty years after its supposed date by a writer of periodical papers, named Addison. Before his time, only one eminent man appears to have

known of it, and that one another poet, named
Dryden, who gives it great praise. Now, Dryden was universally admitted to have been a
genius of the first order, and a celebrated poet;
while Milton, as we have seen, was known only
as a prose writer, and a very prosaic prose writer.
Milton was incapable of writing the *Paradise
Lost;* for, though some shorter poems seem to
have been attributed to him, yet the critic
before referred to (Johnson) says that those who
pretend to like them 'force their judgment into
false approbation of these little pieces, and
prevail on themselves to think that admirable
which is only singular.' He adds of one that
'its diction is harsh, its rhymes uncertain, and
its numbers unpleasing'; and of another, 'In
this poem there is no nature, for there is no
truth.' If, therefore, Milton wrote the shorter
poems, he evidently did not write the longer one.
Youth is the season of poetry. If, in his youth,
he tried to write poetry, and wrote it so badly,
is it possible that, old and blind, after spending
his life in teaching school, making dictionaries,
and writing bitter theological essays, he could
suddenly fall heir to the splendid genius which
irradiates the *Paradise Lost?* Milton could not

have written this poem. But Dryden could. And there was very good reason why Dryden should conceal the fact; for he had been a Puritan, and had become a Catholic. He probably wrote the poem before his change of opinion, and this accounts for the religious views which it contains. He dared not publish it openly under his own name, after becoming a Catholic, and could not bear to suppress it. Nothing remained but to publish it under the name of another; and he selected that of Milton, the Puritan, as an obscure man, to whom it might easily be attributed. This supposition, and only this, accounts for all the facts in the case."

An ingenious critic can always find such arguments as these by which to unsettle the authenticity of any book, no matter how long or how universally ascribed to a particular author. But which is likely to be right,— the individual critic or the universal opinion? Shall we trust the common belief of a period near enough to have the means of knowing the truth, yet distant enough to have had time to gather up all the threads of evidence, or the reasonings and judgment of a man living ten or fifteen centuries after?

Mr. Tayler himself says, "With Irenæus and Tertullian, who mark the transition from the second to the third century, the testimony to the apostolic origin and authority of the Fourth Gospel becomes so clear, express, and full, and the verdict of the Catholic Church respecting it so decisive, that it is quite unnecessary to pursue the line of witnesses any farther." Now, Mr. Tayler supposes it to have been forged or invented after A.D. 135. In less than sixty-five years, then, this false book is universally received as the work of a great apostle who could hardly have been dead fifty years when the Gospel was written, and not a hundred when it was thus universally received as his. Wesley has been dead just about as long as the Apostle John had been dead when the Fourth Gospel was universally ascribed to him. Who can think that a work on religion, essentially differing from Wesley's other teachings, could have been forged a few years after his death, and be now universally accepted in all the Methodist churches of Europe and America as his authentic writing? Yet this is what we are invited to believe concerning the Fourth Gospel.

In deciding such questions, too much weight

is given to the function of criticism, which only judges by the letter. The critical faculty in man is an important one, certainly; but as certainly gives us no knowledge of God or man, of spirit or matter, of law or love. All it can do is to "peep and botanize"; take to pieces the living flower, in order to see how many stamens it has; "murder, to dissect." All the large movements of man's soul are above its reach. It gropes in the dark, like a mole. A single new experience, one inspired impulse, will set aside its most carefully built up array of evidence. It can judge of the future only by the past,— and usually by a very narrow past,— and so is very apt to be deceived.

The French proverb says, "On peut être plus fin qu'un autre, mais pas plus fin que tous les autres." We may believe that our critics in the nineteenth century are very acute; but do they know more about John and his writings than all the Christian churches in the third century together? Possibly there may have been some critical persons there too, and with better means of knowledge than we have. There were Christians *then* who had the power of trying spirits, to see whether they were of God or not;

who could tell if a new Gospel, which was no Gospel, was handed to them, giving an account of their Master wholly different from that which they had been taught by apostolic tradition. According to the critics there was not in all the churches, in the second century, a single man who could look this false John in the face, and tear off his mask, saying, "Jesus I know, Paul I know, Matthew and Mark and Luke I know; but who are you?" But there were men in the churches then, as well as before and after, who had been taught acuteness in the keen discussions of the Jewish and Greek schools, whose wits had been sharpened by rabbinical debates, and who were quite able to see the difference between the Jesus of Luke and the Christ of John. Why, then, was not a single voice raised, in all the churches, against this intruder? The only possible answer is that he came with such guarantees of his character as silenced all question. Holtzmann's book contains a full discussion of the whole question. All that bears on the authority and authorship of the Fourth Gospel has been brought together, and he has not found one writer in the first centuries expressing any doubt of St. John's being the author of the

Fourth Gospel. All that *is* said is in its favor: the only objection is that there is not more. As far as external evidence goes, one should, methinks, be satisfied if it is all one way. But critics whose object is to discredit a book or writer can find fault very easily. Not that they mean to be unfair; but they are students in the school of Baur, and would be more than human if they had not caught the habit there of hinting a fault and hesitating dislike.

The external evidence, *pro* and *con*, may be summed up thus: *All that we have*, in regard to the Fourth Gospel in the first two centuries, is in its favor; and, by the end of the second century, the testimony is so full and plain that even Tübingen critics must admit it to be satisfactory. When one complained that he had not time enough, the reply was not unreasonable,— that he had "all the time there was." To those who want more evidence of the authenticity of the Fourth Gospel, we may in like manner reply that "all the evidence there is, is on that side."

The unanimity of the churches at the end of the second century, in receiving this Gospel as the work of the apostle, is such an inexplicable fact, supposing it to have been forged, that the defenders of this hypothesis are obliged to take the position that Christians were then so uncritical that they were willing to accept as authentic any writing which seemed edifying, without examination or evidence. But this is a mere assumption, contradicted by the facts of the case. Luke, in the preface to his Gospel, already assumes the critical position, though he criticises and denies for the sake of affirming. He rejects the false, in order to retain the true. He tells us that, since so many were undertaking to relate the apostolic traditions concerning Jesus, he wrote his Gospel from very accurate knowledge and the best opportunities, so that Theophilus might have "*certainty*" (ἀσφάλειαν) in his belief. His object was a critical one,— to separate the uncertain and doubtful accounts of Jesus from those well-ascertained and verified. This does not look as if there was no critical judgment in the Church.

We know, moreover, that many apocryphal and doubtful Gospels were in circulation at the beginning. They were not hostile to Christ. They err in the opposite direction. They are zealous to exalt him to the utmost,— to heap miracle on miracle; to paint the lily, and add a perfume to the violet. Why, then, were they rejected? *Love* for Christ might have retained them, but the sense of *truth* rejected them. If, as is assumed, the critical faculty at first was absent, and only blind feeling existed, why were all these well-meant but spurious narratives excluded, one after the other, from the received Scriptures? What has become of the "Gospel of the Infancy," ascribed to the Apostle Thomas; the "Protoevangelium," ascribed to James, brother of the Lord; the "Gospel of the Nativity of Mary," "the Gospel of Nicodemus," and especially the "Gospel to the Hebrews," which once had high authority? The sense of truth in the churches rejected them, one by one,—that spirit of truth which was just as much an element of primitive Christianity as the spirit of love; the spirit of truth which Jesus promised should be given his disciples, and which should "take of his, and show to them."

Eusebius, writing about the year 325, gives an account of the New Testament canon, distinguishing between the books universally received, those received by some and rejected by others, and those generally rejected. This threefold division of accepted, disputed, and spurious certainly shows that the churches in his time had a critical sense in full operation. But, before his time, three eminent writers, all of whom accept as unquestioned the Gospel of John, had shown an active and acute spirit of investigation. The first is Irenæus, disciple of Polycarp, Bishop of Lyons (A.D. 177–202), whom Hase calls "a clear-minded, thoughtful man, of philosophic culture, who opposed the Gnostic speculations with the help of reminiscences taken from his youth, which came in contact with the apostolic age." His testimony to John, the apostle, as author of the Fourth Gospel, the critics admit to be positive and unquestionable. So is that of Tertullian, one of the greatest thinkers and writers in the Church, first a heathen orator and lawyer in Rome (about A.D. 190), whose fiery African nature was joined with the acutest intellect of his time. And, thirdly, Origen (born A.D. 185), learned in all the knowledge of the Alexandrian school, an independent thinker and student. He says that the Gospels of Matthew, Mark, Luke, and John, are the "only undisputed ones in the whole Church of God throughout the world." Origen examines critically all the books of the New Testament, marks the difference of style between the Epistle to the Hebrews and the undisputed writings of the Apostle Paul, and says of it that "who really wrote it God only knows."

By the whole Church, then, including all its great thinkers and writers, at the end of the second century, the authenticity of the Gospel of John is *undisputed.* Also before that time, as far as it is mentioned at all, it is equally undisputed, the only question being why it was not more often mentioned. But the apostolic Fathers were not in the habit of quoting the New Testament writers by name or as authority,— they were too near to their own time,— so that their silence is no argument against their belief in the authenticity of the Gospel.

The external evidence, therefore, concerning the Fourth Gospel, may be thus summed up:—

1. According to Dr. Edwin A. Abbott (Encyclopædia Britannica), Papias and the apostolic Fathers quoted and used it.

2. Every Christian writer, in the first three centuries, who has given the name of its author, has attributed it to the Apostle John.

3. The great writers and critics at the end of the second and beginning of the third century —

Irenæus, Tertullian, Clement, Origen, and afterward Eusebius, who carefully divide the Scriptures into "undoubted, doubtful, and spurious"—all put this Gospel among the undoubted apostolic writings.

4. No serious opposition to the authenticity of this Gospel has arisen until the present time, and among a special class of critics; while others (like Lücke, Godet, Keil, Ewald, De Wette, and Tischendorf) equally acute and free, say that, in regard to external evidence, this Gospel "stands, not in a worse, but in a better position than either the first three Gospels or the writings of Paul." *

We may therefore conclude that, were it not for the objections brought against the contents of the Fourth Gospel, no such doubts of its authenticity would have arisen as now prevail among some learned and candid writers.

Let us therefore examine more carefully the nature of the objections brought on internal grounds.

* De Wette, *Introduction*, etc., § 109.

III.

The internal evidence against the authenticity of the Fourth Gospel may be distributed under three heads: 1. Its difference from the three Synoptics; 2. Its difference from the Apocalypse; 3. Its difference from the writings of Paul.

We begin with the most important of these. The divergence from the first three Gospels relates to the character of Jesus, the events of his life, and its doctrinal teaching.

The first — and, if correct, conclusive — objection against the apostolic origin of the Fourth Gospel is this: *It gives a view of the character of Jesus so different from that of the Synoptics as to constitute another person. The character of Jesus as represented by the Synoptics and that represented by John are contradictory to each other.*

M. Albert Réville (*Revue des Deux Mondes*, liv. de Mai 1, 1866) thus describes this difference: In the first three Gospels, Jesus is a teacher of the Truth; but, in the Fourth, he is the Truth itself. In the Synoptics, he appears as a man; in the Fourth Gospel, as the Word of God. He finds in its author a scholar of Philo, who had appropriated his Platonic theory of the Word, as the indwelling, unuttered thought of God (λόγος ἐνδιάθετος), and as the manifested divine reason (λόγος προφορικός). This Word, according to him, appeared among men as Jesus of Nazareth, and, being essential light, was opposed by the darkness. He attracts to himself all men in whom the light is supreme, and repels the sons of darkness. He calls on all men to believe in himself as "the Way, the Truth, and the Life"; as "the True Vine"; as "the Living Bread which came down from heaven"; as the only open "Door" to God; as the "Well-beloved Son, dwelling in the bosom of the Father." This, says M. Réville, makes an essentially different character from the simple country-rabbi of the Synoptics.

Mr. Tayler's view is the same. He says: "In the first three Gospels, we have the picture, exceedingly vivid and natural, of a great moral and religious reformer, cautiously making his way through the prejudices and misconceptions of his contemporaries, gradually obtaining their confidence, and changing the direction of their hopes. In the Fourth, on the contrary, the unclouded glory of the Son of God shines out complete from the first, and is sustained undiminished till the words 'It is finished' announce its withdrawal from earth."

There is, doubtless, some truth in all this. And yet, if we were disposed to take the opposite view, and say that John chiefly developed the purely *human* side of Jesus, how much we might find to say! John says nothing of the miraculous conception, which appears both in Matthew and Luke; nor of his victory over the doctors in his childhood; nor of his defeat of the devil in his temptation; nor of his influence over demons and evil spirits; nor of his power over the elements of nature, in commanding the winds and waves; nor of the transfiguration; nor of his cursing the fig-tree; nor of the shock of nature at his death, the miraculous darkness, the rending rocks, the dead rising from their graves. And, on the other hand, it is the Gospel of John which furnishes the most purely human traits in the character of Jesus,— which shows him weeping at the grave of Lazarus; which depicts him, weary with his journey, sitting by the well; which shows his need of private friendships, in his love for Martha, Mary, and Lazarus, and the beloved disciple himself; and his sympathy with human cheerfulness, in the water turned to wine.

Still there is no doubt that the Gospel of John gives a quite different view of Christ from that of the Synoptics. The Christ of this is more ideal, reflective, spiritual; the Christ of those, practical, direct, and popular. But Hase well says, "Since a great, unfathomed character must be differently apprehended by those who surround him, according to the difference in the observers and the measure of each man's mind, it follows that John's different view of Jesus proves nothing against the authenticity of his Gospel, unless it could be shown that a higher unity of these diverse views is an impossibility."*

About twenty-five years after the death of Dr. Channing, a meeting was held in Boston to commemorate his character and genius, at which speeches were made by different friends of his, all of whom had known him intimately and well. Yet it was noticed that they gave such different descriptions of his character as almost to contradict each other. Some described him as inaccessible and retiring, others as specially hospitable and easy of approach; some denied to him imagination and poetry, for which others made a peculiar claim; some, in fine, said that he was not a great thinker, while others considered him

* Hase, *Leben Jesu*.

one of the leading intellects of the age. The explanation was that they saw him on different sides of his character.

But the most complete parallel to the divergences between the evangelists is to be found in the widely opposite view of Socrates, as given by Xenophon and Plato. The first represents him as a moral teacher, inculcating self-control, temperance, piety, duty to parents, brotherly love, friendship, diligence, benevolence, and expressly avoiding all ideal themes, as transcending the limits of human knowledge. He was eminently a *practical* man, as thus described in the *Memorabilia*. But, according to Plato, his whole life was passed in speculative inquiries into the essences of things and in transcendental discussions. And, nevertheless, Mr. Grote and other eminent writers consider both accounts authentic and genuine. Mr. Grote says:* "We find, to our great satisfaction, that the pictures given by Plato and Xenophon of their common master are, in the main, accordant; *differing only as drawn from the same original by two authors radically differing in spirit and character*. Xenophon, the man of action, *brings out at length those conversations of Socrates which had a bearing on prac-*

* *History of Greece*, chap. lxviii.

tical conduct, and were calculated to correct vice or infirmity in particular individuals. . . . *Plato leaves out the practical, and consecrates himself to the theoretical Socrates*, whom he divests in part of his identity, in order to enroll him as chief speaker in certain larger theoretical views of his own. *The two pictures, therefore, do not contradict each other, but mutually supply each other's defects, and admit of being blended into one consistent whole.* And, respecting the method of Socrates, as well as the effect of that method on the minds of the hearers, both Xenophon and Plato are witnesses substantially in union; though, here again, the latter has made the method his own, worked it out on a scale of enlargement and perfection, and given it a permanence it could never have derived from its original author, *who talked and never wrote. It is fortunate that our two main witnesses about him, both speaking from personal knowledge, agree to so great an extent.*"

We have italicized the passages which illustrate our present point. As Xenophon and Plato to Socrates, so were the Synoptics and John to Christ. Their two portraits of Jesus " differ only as drawn from the same original by two authors radically differing in spirit and character." The Synoptics, men of action, bring out those sayings of Jesus "which had a bearing on practical conduct." John "leaves out the practical, and consecrates himself to the theoretical" Jesus. "The two pictures, therefore, do not contradict each other, but mutually supply each other's defects."

Have we not also reason to say of Jesus, as Mr. Grote says of Socrates, "It is fortunate that our two main witnesses about him, both speaking from personal knowledge, agree to so great an extent"? Let us see how much the four Gospels have in common. John agrees with the Synoptics in regard to the ministry of John the Baptist as a preparation for that of Jesus; the baptism of Jesus by him; the casting of the Baptist into prison, and subsequent return of Jesus into Galilee; the healing of the centurion's servant; the feeding of the five thousand; the walking on the sea; Peter's profession of faith; the anointing by Mary; the entry of Christ into Jerusalem at the last Passover; the fact of the cleansing of the Temple; the fact of the supper; the fall of Peter foretold by Jesus; Gethsemane; the betrayal by Judas; the examination before the high priest; the denial by

Peter; the examination by Pilate; the accusation and condemnation; the abuse by the soldiers; the crucifixion; the burial; the resurrection; the appearances in Jerusalem.

Moreover, passages occur in the Synoptics, in exact harmony with those in John, in which Jesus is represented not merely as a teacher of Truth, but as himself the Truth and Life. What is there in John more striking of this kind than the passage in Matthew (xi., 28), "Come unto me, all ye that labor and are heavy laden, and I will give you rest"; or the preceding passage, "No man knows who the Son is but the Father, or who the Father is but the Son, and he to whom the Son shall reveal him"? What vaster claim is there in John than that in Matthew (xxviii., 18), "All power is given to me in heaven and earth"; or the picture of himself (Matt. xxv., 31) as the future judge of all the nations of the world, accompanied by the angels? And, on the other hand, John's Gospel asserts, as fully as those of the Synoptics, the human limitations and dependence of Jesus. When accused of arrogating to himself the name of God, he claims only that of a son, appealing with entire humility to the Old Testament use of language (John xvi., 33-36). He ascribes exclusive honor to the Father only (John vii., 18), and professes to do nothing of himself (John v., 30).

IV.

Passing from the picture of the character of Jesus to the story of events in his career, we first encounter this fact: The Synoptics place all the first part of the life of Jesus in Galilee, and say nothing of his going to Jerusalem before the last Passover. John, on the other hand, mentions several visits to Jerusalem, at different festivals. But it is in the highest degree probable that Jesus complied with the national custom in going to the feasts; and that he took occasion, while there, to talk with the leaders of different parties, and test their state of mind in respect to his mission. He went only as a private man on each of these occasions, as is stated in regard to one of them (John vii., 10, οὐ φανερῶς, ἀλλ' ὡς ἐν κρυπτῷ,—"not publicly, but as it were privately"). In accordance with this, he avoided working miracles; or, if he could not refuse the suppliant, he adopted some method by which he withdrew from observation. This we suppose to have been his reason for anointing the eyes of the blind man with clay, and telling him to wash in the pool of Siloam. The man did not discover that he was healed till he had gone and washed off the clay (John ix., 1–7). So, in the healing of the impotent man, Jesus avoided publicity (John v., 13). He spoke of himself to the Jews as being sent by God, and speaking what was given him to say; but he nowhere openly claimed to be the Messiah. He spoke of the Messiah frequently under the title of "the Son," and described his qualities; but he refused the request of his brethren, that he should "show himself to the world" (John vii., 3–6), on the ground that his time had not yet come. This invitation indicates plainly that he did not appear as publicly in Jerusalem as in Galilee. The Synoptics, therefore, describing only his public life, and perhaps not having gone with him to Jerusalem on these visits, say nothing of them; but John speaks of them, because of the conversations which took place there. It is probable that, meeting at the feast men of a deeper insight and higher culture than in Galilee, Jesus spoke to them more plainly of his idea of the Messiah; and these are the conversations which John narrates. Questions constantly arose as to whether he were the Christ or not, but Jesus himself delayed any claim to that title. Undoubtedly, he asserts a great mission: He is the light of the world. He is from above. If any man thirst, let him come to him and drink. His day was seen by Abraham: therefore, he existed in the divine purpose before Abraham. But still he would not say plainly that he was the Christ (John x., 24). His sheep would know his voice, without any such claim.

This, we think, sufficiently explains the silence of the Synoptics in regard to these visits to Jerusalem. Jesus went alone, or with only one or two of his disciples, as a private Jew, to the national festivals. For this reason, the Synoptics omit mention of them; but John, who may have gone with his Master at these times, found sufficient interest in the conversations to record them as he was able to remember them.

A great difficulty is made of the omission, by the Synoptics, of any mention of the raising of Lazarus. Why they omit it cannot now be known. Lazarus and his family were the objects of hatred to the authorities at Jerusalem (John xii., 10); and, living so near to their enemies, it was perhaps not best to call attention to them. Perhaps only one or two of the disciples had gone with Jesus on this occasion to Bethany; and the others, hearing of the miracle from those who were there, might not have thought it more important than those in their own narrations. Perhaps— but why multiply suggestions? Who can answer such questions? Why does Luke alone relate the parables of the Good Samaritan, the Pharisee and Publican, and the Prodigal Son? Any explanation is better than to suppose this exquisitely natural and touching narrative an invention. If nature and truth ever put their seal to a story, it is here. The little picture of domestic life at Bethany, as it appears in Luke (x., 38-42), prepares the way for the narrative in John. The characters of Martha and Mary are in keeping in both narratives. The active sister, in Luke's picture, is the one who comes first, in John's account, to meet Jesus. The one who sat at his feet, in the story of Luke, is the sister whose tender gratitude violates all utilitarian considerations in the gift of ointment, as narrated by all four evangelists. But, though Matthew and Mark tell this last story, they do not mention the name of Mary,—

for the same reason apparently, whatever it was, which caused their silence in regard to the raising of Lazarus. Martha, again, who in Luke (x., 40) was cumbered with much serving, true to her active and useful tendencies appears also in John (xii., 2) as serving on this other occasion. All these little traits combine in a perfect picture; and all are in harmony with the story of the raising of Lazarus, which, the more it is read, seems ever more real.

The difference between the Synoptics and the Fourth Gospel, as regards the last supper, is sometimes made a strong reason for denying the authenticity of the latter. According to the first three Gospels, Jesus eats the Passover with his disciples on the regular Jewish festival (14th Nisan), and then, after the Paschal supper, institutes his own memorial feast. He is crucified on the next day (15th Nisan), Friday; and the bodies are taken down immediately, so as not to interfere with the Sabbath. Jesus lies in his grave on Saturday (the Sabbath), and rises on Sunday, the first day of the week.

But, according to John, the supper (identified by the sop given to Judas [xiii., 26] and the prediction concerning the cock to Peter [xiii.,

38]) was the previous day (13th Nisan): since John speaks of it as "before the feast of the Passover" (xiii., 1); since Judas goes out, as was thought, "to buy the things needed for the feast" (xiii., 29); since, on the next day, the Jews were still to eat the Passover (xviii., 28); and since it was the preparation for it (xix., 14, 31).

There is one method, however, of explaining this difficulty, which perhaps has never been fully presented, and which we submit for the consideration of our readers. John has been supposed to have written his Gospel when he was quite an old man, about A.D. 80 or 90. We must not think of him as composing it in the way men write purely literary works,— as one connected whole. He wrote it, or, more probably, dictated it, as he was able, in fragments and parts. From time to time, he wrote down or dictated some particular passage of his Master's life or some special conversation. Afterward, they were put together in the best way either by himself or by some one else after his death. There are many indications of this fragmentary manner of composition in the Gospel itself. There is no natural connection in the narrative. Often, an artificial connection is supplied, as though the amanuensis had asked the apostle, "When did this happen?" and he had replied, "That happened the next day" (John i., 29), "this was the next day after" (i., 35), "and this, I recollect, was the day after that" (i., 43). "It took about two days to go to Galilee, so this must have been on the third day" (ii., 1). The amanuensis may be supposed to have asked, "How long did he stay there?" and been answered, "Not many days" (ii., 12). The whole impression given in reading the Gospel is as if the aged apostle had been surrounded by a group of younger Christians, who asked him questions about his recollections of Jesus, and wrote down his answers. "Tell us," they would say, "about Nicodemus"; or "Tell us of the Christ's conversation at the last supper"; or "Tell us all you can remember of his conversations with the Jews at the feasts." So, when he told them about Jesus washing his disciples' feet, they probably asked, "When was this?" and he answered, "Before the feast of the Passover." But, in arranging the different papers on which were written down these conversations and incidents, they may have sometimes misplaced them.

Let us suppose the Gospel to be printed as a collection of separate reminiscences, and not a continuous whole; and, instead of being divided into chapters and verses, to be numbered Recollections 1, 2, 3, which the reader is at liberty to arrange as he pleases,— what will be the result as to the supper?

First, it would appear that the whole passage contained in John xiii. and John xiv. (with an exception to be noticed presently) is an account, not of the Paschal feast at which the supper was instituted; but, as Lightfoot and others have supposed, of a supper which Jesus and his apostles took in company a day or two before. This would account for the introductory phrase, "Before the feast of the Passover," and for the closing summons, otherwise inexplicable, "Arise; let us go hence."

All readers have doubtless been struck with this last sentence. Why did Jesus say, "Arise; let us go hence," and then go on with a long series of remarks, extending through sixty verses, and closing with the prayer in chap. xvii.? If he arose to go, and then changed his mind, why did John record at all the proposal to leave the room at that moment, which thus became insignificant? The simple and natural explanation is that they *did* leave the room, and close the conversation then; and what follows in the next three chapters is the recollection of another conversation at another time, not sufficiently distinguished by the compiler of these Johannine fragments. This second conversation (chaps. xv., xvi., xvii.) probably belongs to the institution of the supper, and is a supplement to the account of that transaction as told by the Synoptics. Its opening words, "I am the true vine," connect themselves naturally with the words (recorded by Matthew and Mark), "I will not drink henceforth of this fruit of the vine, till the day when I drink it new with you in my Father's kingdom." For "I am the true vine," etc. The "*new* wine" is thus explained to be the new communion,—inward, and not outward,—by which Jesus was to be no longer with them as a companion and friend, but in them as a life and inspiration. The connection is then complete. The principal subject of the first conversation, introduced by the washing of the feet, was their duty to serve and help each other after he was gone. The chief topic of the second conversation, introduced by the Lord's Supper, was their communion with him and common life in him. The only difficulty in this explanation is the passage (John xiii., 21–38) containing the account of the sop given to Judas, and the prediction of Peter's fall and the cock-crow. These, according to the Synoptics, belong to the second conversation at the Paschal supper, on Thursday evening, and, if so, have been misplaced, and inserted by mistake here. This mistake was probably occasioned by verse 18, in which Jesus alluded to his betrayer on the first evening, but less distinctly than on the second. On the other hand, the passage in Luke (xxii., 24–30) seems evidently to belong to the first conversation, and to the washing of feet. With this alteration, the chief difficulty is removed.

We may say, in fact, that by this change the *whole* difficulty of the chronology of Passion Week is removed. For the passage in John (xviii., 28) about the Jews not going into the judgment-hall lest they should be defiled, "but that they might eat the Passover," is explained by John xix., 14, which calls this day the "*preparation* for the Passover" (compared with verse 31, which makes it the preparation for the Paschal Sabbath, which was the great day of the feast; and also compared with Mark xv., 42, and Luke xxiii., 54, "because it was the preparation, — that is, the day before the Sabbath"). The Jews would not go into Pilate's hall, but not because that would prevent them from *eating the Paschal supper* that evening; for it would not have done so. If the Paschal Supper was still to be eaten that evening, then the feast had not begun; and going into Pilate's hall would not have defiled them. So Lightfoot declares, and there can be no higher authority for Hebrew usages. "To eat the Passover" (John xviii., 28) he understands to refer to the feast on the second evening of the Paschal season, when, as the festival was actually in progress, the Jews would have become ceremonially defiled by entering the Roman prætorium.

The difference between the Fourth Gospel and the Revelation is so great, say many critics, that, if John, the apostle, wrote the one, he could not have written the other. To this, we reply:—

1. The differences are more superficial than essential, rather those which touch the form than such as affect the substance. Suppose the Apocalypse to have been written in the midst of the horrors of the first persecutions, when

the writer was comparatively young, and all the passionate fire of his heart and imagination was thrown into this ecstatic vision; and that the Gospel was dictated thirty years after, when he had meditated deeply, and when a long Christian experience had purified his soul,—then there need not be any such difficulty in supposing one man the author of both. The difference between them is not so great as between Swedenborg's *Algebra* and his *Heaven and Hell;* his treatise on *Docks, Sluices, and Salt-works,* and the *Arcana Cœlestia;* his large folio volumes on *Mines and Mining* and his *Apocalypse Revealed.* Baur himself finds points of contact between the Fourth Gospel and the Apocalypse, though he thinks that the writer of the Gospel purposely imitated the latter book.* "It cannot be denied," says Baur, "that the evangelist wished to give his book the authority of the apostle who wrote the Apocalypse, and so assumed the same intellectual position. There is not merely an outward support in the name of the highly revered apostle, but there are not wanting many internal resemblances between the Gospel and the Apocalypse. In fact, one must admire the deep genial sympathy and the delicate skill which

* Baur, *Das Christenthum*, etc. Tübingen, 1860.

the writer has shown in finding in the Apocalypse elements which could be developed into the loftier and larger views of the evangelist. He has thus spiritualized the Book of Revelation into a Gospel." The amount of which is that Baur does not find the Gospel so essentially different from the Apocalypse as Mr. Tayler and others do.

2. But, if we must choose between the Apocalypse and the Gospel as apostolic writings, every thing should lead us to surrender the first. The authorship of the Gospel was never doubted by antiquity: that of the Apocalypse was. At the end of the second century, when the Christian scriptures were distributed into those which were unquestioned, those which were doubtful, and those which were spurious, the Gospel was placed in the first division, and the Book of Revelation in the second.

One objection urged against the Fourth Gospel is its anti-Jewish tone of thought. Granting this in the main, we yet find such expressions as that used to the Samaritan woman,— "We know what we worship; for salvation is from the Jews." But it is thought that, if the apostle wrote the Apocalypse, which is strongly Jewish, he could not so soon after have changed his tone so entirely. But is the writer of the Apocalypse so Jewish, when a part of his object is to announce judgments on Jerusalem? And, again, why may not John have risen above his Jewish tendencies into a universal Christianity, since Paul passed through the same change? It is said that, if Jesus had really taught as anti-Jewish a gospel as is represented by John, the struggle between Paul and his opponents could never have taken place. But this is to ignore the universal tendency in men and sects to notice only that which is in accord with their own prejudices.

V.

We have seen Holtzmann's account of the latest opinions on this question. The earlier history of belief in regard to this Gospel is as follows. It is supposed to be referred to by Luke and Mark (De Wette). The apostolic Fathers do not refer to it directly, but Eusebius tells us that Papias made use of testimonies from the First Epistle of John. Papias had been a hearer of John in his youth, and was an Asiatic bishop in the middle of the second century. Justin Martyr, in the middle of the second century; Tatian; and the Clementine Homilies contain passages so strikingly like those in the Gospel that they appear to have been taken from it.* Johannic formulas are found in the Gnostic writings, about A.D. 140. The first distinct declaration, however, that the Apostle John was the author of the Fourth Gospel comes about A.D. 180, from Theophilus of Antioch, who quotes the passage, " In the beginning was the Word." After this, it is continually quoted and referred to by all the great writers at the end of the second and beginning of the third century,— as Irenæus, Bishop of Lyons, Clement of Alexandria, Tertullian of Carthage, and Origen. None of these scholars express any doubt concerning the authorship of the Gospel; and their quotations from it are so numerous that, if it were lost, it might almost be reconstructed from their writings.

The first doubts of the authenticity of the Gospel (unless we consider its rejection by the *Alogi* to be based on critical reasons) are brought forward in the seventeenth century, in England, by

---

*See Ezra Abbot's *Authorship of the Fourth Gospel*, in which, after the most thorough critical inquiry, he concludes that it must have been quoted by Justin, and made a part of Tatian's *Diatessaron*.

some unknown writer, and were refuted by the great scholar, Le Clerc. After this there followed a silence of a hundred years, when the attack was renewed in 1792 by another Englishman,— Evanson. Nothing more was heard on the subject; and the replies to these doubts seemed to have satisfied all minds, when Bretschneider, in 1820, made another assault in the *Probabilia*. He was replied to by a multitude of critics, and afterward retracted his opinion, and admitted that his objections had been fully answered.* No other opponent to the authenticity of the Gospel appeared till 1835, when Dr. Strauss, in his Life of Jesus, renewed the attack, and was answered by Neander, Tholuck, Hase, Lücke, and others. Dr. Strauss, moved by these replies, retracted his doubts in 1838, but advanced them again in 1840.†

Then arose the famous school of Tübingen, from which all the recent attacks on the Gospel have been derived. Mr. Tayler and other writers, both French and English, who have taken the negative side, seem only followers of Baur and Zeller. Dr. F. C. Baur, a truly great man, began his immense labors with a work on

* *Handbuch der Dogmatik*, § 34, note.
† Réville, *Revue des Deux Mondes*, May, 1886.

mythology, published in 1824, and continued them by several other works, published every year, in different departments of theology, until his death. His vast learning, great industry, acute insight, and love of truth make his writings very valuable. The integrity of his mind was such that, even when carrying on a controversy, he seems more like an inquirer than a disputant. Even when differing from his conclusions, one derives very valuable suggestions from his views. One characteristic of the criticism of Baur is his doctrine of *intention*. He ascribes to the New Testament writers a special aim, which leads them to exaggerate some facts and omit or invent others. Everywhere, he seeks for an intention, for some private or party purpose which colors the narrative, and in the present instance ascribes to the writer of the Fourth Gospel the deliberate purpose of passing himself off as the apostle, in order to impose on the Christian Church his doctrine of the Logos. This attack roused new defenders of the Gospel, among whom the most conspicuous have been Ewald and Tischendorf.

Some critics, who reject the apostolic origin of this Gospel, acquit the writer of any purpose of deceiving his readers. But if we assume, with Baur, that the Fourth Gospel is a work of fiction, written in the second century, I think we must go further, and agree with him that it was intended to appear as coming from the apostle. Else why were so many names of persons and places introduced, well known to the readers of the other evangelists? Why were the real facts of the life of Jesus so skilfully interwoven in the narrative? Why the assertion in regard to its being written by John, "This is the disciple who wrote these things, and testifieth of these things; and we know that his testimony is true"? The Fourth Gospel, if not an authentic narrative, is the most remarkable and only entirely successful literary imposition on record. It has deceived the whole Church for eighteen hundred years.

VI.

It is a remark of Lord Bacon that "the harmony of a science, supporting each part the other, is and ought to be the true and brief confutation and suppression of the smaller sorts of objections." This sagacious observation indicates another method of deciding this question.

Of these two views, the one attributing the Gospel to the Apostle John, the other to an anonymous writer in the middle of the second century, — which gives us the most harmonious and consistent story? Let us look at each opinion in reference to this question.

According to the received opinion of the Church, John, the apostle, composed this Gospel at Ephesus, in his old age. As years and thought and intense religious life changed Swedenborg, the miner and engineer, into the great visionary and mystic, so years and thought and inward inspiration had changed the Jewish disciple, first into a visionary, and later into a mystic. In his lonely exile at Patmos, his vivid imagination had made a series of pictures, representing symbolically the struggle of Christianity with the Jewish and Roman power, and its ultimate triumph. "Every man," says Coleridge, "is a Shakspere in his dreams." Day by day, these dreams came to John; and he wrote down the visions, and they were collected into the Book of Revelation. When he returned to active life and the service of the Seven Churches of Asia, he came in contact with a new order of thought, for which he had a natural affinity.

This was the Platonic and Mystic school of Philo, which laid the greatest stress on the distinction between the spirit and the letter, between the hidden and revealed Deity, and between the Logos, or reason of God, and the same light shining in the soul of man. Contact with this school ripened in the mind of the apostle the mystic tendency peculiar to him,—for there is a true mysticism as well as a false. The apostle, mystical, in the best sense, loved to look on spiritual facts as substantial realities. Hence, his fondness for such expressions as Truth, Life, Light, Spirit, and his conception of the Messiah as the Son, Well-beloved, and dwelling in the bosom of the Father. His recollections of Jesus reposed especially on those deeper conversations in which his Master's thought took this direction. These conversations had been more frequent at Jerusalem, where Jesus had encountered minds of a higher culture: therefore, John loved to repeat these. Then, in his old age, when the oral traditions, which made the staple of apostolic preaching, had taken form in the Synoptic Gospels, the disciples of John begged him to write for them, or dictate to them, these other relations concerning Jesus, with which they had become familiar.

So they were repeated, and afterward collected in a Gospel "according to John"; and its universal reception in the Christian Church by so many different schools of thought, as early as the middle of the last half of the second century, shows that there could be no doubt of its origin. In its essence, it is a true picture of Jesus, seen on one side of his life and doctrine. Some errors of expression and of collocation of passages may have occurred; and sometimes the mind of John himself may have colored the teachings of his Master. But in the main it is a true picture, not of John only, but also of Christ.

Let us now look at the other explanation, as proposed by Baur, Albert Réville, and others.

This theory assumes that, while the whole body of apostles and early disciples were teaching to the churches that view of Jesus and his doctrine which finally took form in the first three Gospels, another and a wholly different school of opinion was being developed in the Church, independently of the apostles. This school was derived from the Alexandrian philosophy, and yet grew up within the Christian Church. It held firmly to the Logos doctrine of Philo, but needed some point of contact with the teachings of Christ.

This led an unknown writer, in the first half of the second century, to write another Gospel, and introduce into it Jesus teaching the doctrines of the Alexandrian school. The narrations peculiar to this Gospel are held to be inventions,— the story of the woman of Samaria, of Nicodemus, of the marriage at Cana, of the man born blind, the raising of Lazarus, the washing of the disciples' feet, the wonderful descriptions of the last days of Jesus, of the arrest, trial, crucifixion, and resurrection. The sublime teachings of this Gospel are due to this unknown writer: the sayings which have helped to change the world were pure inventions. Jesus never said, "God is a spirit, and those who worship him must worship him in spirit and in truth": our false gospeller put it in his mouth. Jesus never uttered the sublime prayer with his disciples, recorded in the seventeenth chapter,— a prayer which has touched the hearts of so many generations. This also was composed in cold blood, in order to make the story more interesting. The tender words from the cross, " Woman, behold thy son!" and " Behold thy mother!" are an unauthorized interpolation in that sacred agony. Mary's recognition of her risen Master by the tone in which he spoke her name, and the "Rabboni!" with its untranslatable world of feeling,— these, too, are the adroit fabrications of our apocryphist. And this new Gospel, thus invented, is accepted, without a question, doubt, or hesitation, in every part of the Christian Church. Other books of Scripture they lingered over, doubtful of their right to enter the canon. But this bold-faced forgery all parties, all sects, all schools, all the great theologians and scholars, accepted at once, without a question; and this, too, when it was written with the express purpose of teaching them what they did not already believe, and which was in direct opposition to their authentic and received Gospels! Simply to state such a position is to show its weakness.

VII.

In the passage John v., 17–47, there seems, at first sight, a self-assertion on the part of Jesus not in harmony with his calm, impersonal teaching in the Synoptic Gospels. But, if we look below the letter and phrase, we shall find two ideas intertwined throughout, both of which are fully expressed in Matthew, Mark, and Luke. One is the conviction that God is his Father, in which conviction he finds pure insight, the sense of divine love, and ability to raise mankind into spiritual life. The other is the constantly repeated declaration that this knowledge, power, and love are continually derived from a higher source; that he can do nothing of himself; that he is a son of God only while depending on the Father. He is thus teaching, in another form, exactly what we find declared in the Sermon on the Mount. Throughout that discourse, Jesus speaks with the same irresistible authority of conviction. The difference is that in John he claims for *himself* what in Matthew he claims *for his disciples*. He asserts for them that they are children of the Father, that they therefore can and ought to be filled with his spirit, to be perfect as he is perfect, to forgive as he forgives. They are the salt of the earth, the light of the world. They are to love as God loves, and to be a blessing to their enemies as well as their friends. And this will come to them by living in dependence on their Father in heaven, asking and receiving, seeking and finding. The self-assertion of Jesus in John is no greater than when (Matt. xi., 28) he declares his power to give rest to all the sorrows of earth, than when (Matt. xxv., 31) he represents himself as the judge of mankind, or (Matt. xxviii., 18) asserts that all power is given to him in heaven and earth. In all cases, it is the expression of the same law,— that entire obedience to divine truth, with perfect dependence on the divine will, gives to the soul a fulness of insight, power, and love. If, then, we see that the central thought in John and the Synoptics is the same, we may willingly admit that the phraseology in the Fourth Gospel is colored by the idiosyncrasy of the writer, and does not wholly represent the transparent clearness of the original expressions of Jesus. Such is probably the fact. The thoughts and the life of Jesus sank deep into the soul of John, but were sometimes reproduced in his own language. Some men can remember words more easily than ideas; but, with others, the words pass away while the thoughts remain. If the latter was the characteristic of our apostle's mind, it will largely account for the difference between himself and the Synoptics, in regard to their reports of the teaching of Christ. The deeper thoughts escaped the apprehension of the latter, but the practical teaching of Jesus they have reported verbally. John gives us the profounder thoughts and loftier visions of his Master's soul, but often slightly disguised in terminology of his own. He was, like Paul, a faithful minister of the spirit, if not of the letter, of the new covenant.

It may be said, "If we have not the very language of Jesus, how can we know what he himself really taught, and what belongs to his reporter?" This difficulty is not so great as it at first appears. If we have once become acquainted with the mind of Christ, we shall be able to distinguish what is in harmony with it. The Gospel cannot contradict itself. The merely critical understanding is like the natural man who receiveth not the things of the spirit of God. They are spiritually discerned. He who has the spirit of his Master judgeth all things.

This appears to be the doctrine taught by Jesus himself in his conversation with Nicodemus. Nicodemus rested his belief in the authority of Jesus on his wonderful works, on the signs and miracles. Jesus refused to be accepted on that ground, and declared spiritual insight necessary, in order to see the kingdom of God. He intimates that, by such methods of reasoning from outward facts, only an outward and earthly Messiah can be inferred. That which is born of the flesh is flesh. Jesus spoke to the Jews from a profound spiritual insight, and they received not his witness. Except they saw signs and wonders, they would not believe. This refusal by Jesus to accept a belief based on miracles accords with such sayings in the Synoptics as that "an evil generation seeketh for a sign." According to Nicodemus, faith in Jesus must rest on his miracles. According to Jesus, the miracles must rest on faith. "He did not many mighty works there, because of their unbelief." Thus, we find, both in John and the Synoptics, a revelation of the mind of Christ in regard to this point.

In this conversation with Nicodemus and what follows, it has always been found difficult to discriminate between the sayings of Jesus and that portion which comes from John. The method we suggest is the best way of solving the problem. Find what part of the passage is in harmony with the mind of Christ, and we cannot be far wrong.

The conversation with the woman of Samaria carries with it the stamp of reality throughout. As, in the Synoptics, Jesus is called "the friend of publicans and sinners," so here he appears again as the friend of a sinner. As, in the Synoptics, he lays the highest stress on that prayer which is not to be seen of man, so here he teaches that those who worship must worship the Father in spirit and truth. As, in the Synoptics, he is found in kindly and helpful relations with Romans and Phœnicians, so here he makes himself the friend of a Samaritan. Besides the realistic truth of the narrative, we see that its substance is in harmony with the mind of Christ.

The strong affection which Jesus felt for his disciples, and his constant habit of identifying himself with them, is apparent in the Synoptic narratives. "He that receiveth you receiveth me; and he that receiveth me receiveth him that sent me." This love reaches its highest expression in John, especially in the last conversations and in the sublimity of the closing prayer. In these final hours, the human affection is glorified in an immortal love. "I in them, and thou in me, that they may be perfectly one." In this, as in other instances, we see that, while the fundamental thought is the same in all the evangelists, it reaches its most profound and elevated form in the Fourth Gospel.

The Fourth Gospel has been claimed as containing the strongest proofs of the divinity of Jesus. Certainly, the spiritual element in the Master is most highly emphasized in this; but it is also certain that his pure humanity and absolute dependence on God are also as strongly pronounced. It is asserted that the supernatural nature of Jesus is plainly taught by John. But Dr. Edwin A. Abbott calls attention to the fact that this Gospel, even more than the others, brings out the purely human element in Jesus; as when (John x., 33) he puts his position as Son of God by the side of that of the Jewish prophets. Dr. Abbott adds that the special privilege of pre-existence disappears in the words, "Did this man sin, or his fathers, that he was born blind?" and says that the works of Jesus are represented by John as conformed to unchanging law, and not as the result of supernatural interposition.

Our conclusions in regard to the source of the Fourth Gospel are, therefore, these:—

It is very improbable that it should have proceeded from a writer in the second century, outside of Christian tradition, and importing into it a non-Christian element. Such an apocryphal Gospel would not have been received without leaving marked traces of opposition. No such traces exist in history. The apocryphal Gospels which have come down to us show no such creative power, or harmony with the spirit of Jesus, as is found in the Fourth Gospel; and their speedy rejection indicates that the Church was watchful, and ready to detect any such pretenders.

It is also improbable that the Fourth Gospel, in the form in which it has come to us, should have been written by John himself. Its divergence from the Synoptics, as pointed out above, is evidence of this.

The traditions concerning Jesus, contained in this venerable document, must have come from John, since it was received by the churches as "the Gospel according to John." But these communications, made from time to time to his disciples, were perhaps collected after his death, and put in shape by one of them, with the purpose of being used as a support for the high spiritual view of Jesus and his teaching, which they had received from John's lips during his life.

Our conclusions as to the contents of the Fourth Gospel are as follows:—

One part of the contents of this work produces, in a slightly different form, the Synoptic traditions. Some of these have been already mentioned.

Another part of the Gospel gives traditions concerning the life and teachings of Jesus *not* contained in the Synoptics. Many of these are of great value, giving a larger, deeper, and higher view of the character of Jesus than can be derived from the other evangelists. John, by his spiritual constitution, was able to appropriate and retain some of the loftiest elements in the soul of his Master, which escaped the less sensitive susceptibilities of his companions.

Another element in this Gospel is that which comes from the mind of John himself. His words are often so blended with those of Jesus that the only distinguishing test is the analogy of faith, or the mind of Christ. What accords with *that* is from him: whatever is discordant belongs to a lower source. When particles of iron are mixed with sand, if we move them with a magnet, the iron adheres to it, and can thus be separated from the rest. He who has the mind of Christ, he who has become familiar with the spirit of the Master, can often attain a like power of discrimination.

There may finally remain a small residuum, coming from the imperfect insight or memory of those who reported John's teaching. An example of this is given above, which, if accepted, removes the difficulty of the time of the Passover.

We do not profess to have reached the final solution of this interesting problem, but we hope that this essay tends in the direction toward such a solution. Space would not allow of stating all the arguments against the Johannine origin of this Gospel. But we have noticed the principal ones,— those based both on external and internal grounds. The result of this examination has brought us to the belief that no historic fact of authorship stands on a firmer basis than this, and that the long-received opinion of the Christian Church is not likely to be essentially altered. Were it otherwise, it would seem to us one of the greatest misfortunes which could befall Christianity. The Fourth Gospel will be studied more thoroughly and affectionately, not as a perfectly literal transcript of a divine revelation, but as full of the highest spiritual life, and as bringing us more closely than any other into communion with the inmost mind and heart of Jesus.

www.ingramcontent.com/pod-product-compliance
Lightning Source LLC
Chambersburg PA
CBHW021201100426
42735CB00046B/1911